The Book of Daniel.ipp

God's Word to Us In Poetic Prose

by

Larry N. Locha
M.Ed., B.B.A.

ISBN 978-0-6151-8021-2

Acknowledgements

I'd like to acknowledge several friends who took notice of this work and have expressed positive comments concerning its content. My friend, and former fellow comrade in arms (United States Army), Rev. (Dr.) Charles Alkula, has commented on numerous occasions to its relevance, for which I am deeply grateful. My good friend, Dr. Ron Sones, had inspiring comments and words of encouragement for me.

Credit is given to Christian Theological Seminary, Paul Abramson, and R. Gibson (thebiblerevival.com and breadsite.org) for allowing use of various clipart images from their websites.

I'd also like to thank members of Shearer Hills Baptist Church Adult VI Bible Study Class for allowing me to share with them this poetic form of God's Holy Word.

"The prince of the eunuchs brought them in before Nebuchadnezzar."— *Dan.* i. 18.

Daniel 1

In Judah, King Jehoiakim's reign
Came down in shame.

And God's holy land, Israel,
Into the hands of Babylon's King
Nebuchadnezzar, fell.

Objects were taken from the sacred Temple of
God,
And with the chief palace official, Ashpenaz, to
Babylon trod.

Also, good-looking young men from each royal or
noble family which was wealthy
Were taken captive, as they'd be great thinkers
and learners, as well as being healthy.

Daniel, Hananiah, Mishael, and Azariah, names
of three captives of this foe,
Had to have their names changed to
Belteshazzar, Shadrach, Meshach, and
Abednego.

The king assigned the best wines to drink and
the richest food to eat,
Hoping in three years they'd be advisors at the
royals' feet.

Daniel, however, decided not to partake of the
king's offer of wine and food,
For defiling himself in God's eyes would be rude.

He asked for other food instead.
But the attendant said the king had already instructed.

Daniel, though, was able to convince a test
To see after 10 days who'd be the best.

To take a look at the matter
To see who would be fatter.

So without further delay,
God allowed it Daniel's way.

And after the 10 days, Daniel, Shadrach,
Meshach, and Abednego looked mighty fine,
Having not partaken of the king's rich food and wine.

While the overseer then ordered all to eat only vegetables,
God anointed these four academic 'exceptionals.'

They all became knowledgeable in language, literature, and science,
And Daniel learned he could understand the meanings of visions and dreaming clients.

The training period ended when the king
Ordered the four friends to come and show off their intellectual bearing.

Impressed by their skill,
The king appointed them to his will.

Daniel stayed true to his best,
And God's sovereignty provided him comfort and
rest.

Daniel 2

One night, Nebuchadnezzar had a disturbing
dream about which nothing he knew.

So he called all his magicians; he called all his
enchanters; he called all his sorcerers and
astrologers, too.

The king ordered them tell him his dream and
interpret it; otherwise, they'd all be through.

Of course, no man alive could possibly follow the
orders the king blew.

Nonetheless, the decree issued to kill all wise
men, including Daniel and his three friends,
proved the king mean as a shrew.

Arioch, upon these four, was the one to do.

But when Arioch met him, Daniel was informed
of the king's cue.

Daniel then asked for only a moment or two.

He prayed and prayed to God until he was blue,

And God revealed to him what's about to brew.

Daniel gave thanks and praises to god for all to
Him is due.

When Arioch appeared again, Daniel stated that
in lieu
Of the ordered deaths, he could give the king
revelation anew.

Whew!!

So Daniel was quickly ushered off to forgo the
deadly scheme,
And went to interpret Nebuchadnezzar's dream.

This is what Daniel said
About the dream of the king as he lay in bed:

"First," he said, "no man alive could tell kings
The secrets of such visionary things.

"The dream of your sleep
Provides you a future peep

"Of things to come.
That's it in sum!"

"But God chose me for no particular reason to
tell you His plan,
Because He wants you to understand.

"A statue with a head of gold
 Will take hold.

"Of silver will be its arms and chest.
And the rest?

8

"Bronze belly and each thigh
Of the statue on high.

"Statue with iron legs; and feet of mixed iron and
clay,
Upon foundation display.

"But as you watched, a rock was cut,
From a mountain, leaving a deep rut.

"The rock struck the feet of iron mixed with clay,
Tumbling, crushing them out of the way.

"The rock tumbled the statue to pieces as small
as chaff,
Leaving many without a laugh.

"A rock which took the statue to bare
Will forever represent God, His mountain there.

"Representing your kingdom with the gold head
on top,
Shows that yours is second to none, no other
can stop.

"The next kingdom after the end of yours,"
Daniel expressed,
Is shown by silver arms and silver chest.

"The next to rule the world on high
Has bronze for the belly and each thigh.

"The leg for the fourth kingdom of this statue
jumble
Made of iron, also hard to crumble.

"And the last kingdom, of feet as they lay,
Was made from a mixture of iron and clay.

"Through alliances and intermarriages formed
To strengthen and weather any upcoming kind
of storm."

King Nebuchadnezzar continued listening, all
ears,
Hoping Daniel's forecast could settle all fears.

Daniel continued his description
Of Nebuchadnezzar's dreaming fascination.

"The rock, representing the reign of the God of
heaven,
Will crush all earthly kingdoms like bread un-
leaven."

"All these things will be true,
The will of God left for you to construe."

At the end of Daniel's observation
King Nebuchadnezzar bowed at Daniel's feet in
honor of the God of his explanation.

"Your God is the God of gods," the king said,
"the revealer of my misery and mystery.
You and your friends will be now appointed high
positions within my dynasty."

Nebuchadnezzar's Statue. By James Tissot
(1836-1902)

"Shadrach, Meshach, and Abednego in the Fiery Furnace" by Gustave Doré

Dan 3:28 *Then* Nebuchadnezzar spake, and said, Blessed *be* the God of Shadrach, Meshach, and Abednego, who hath sent his angel, ... that they might not serve nor worship any god, except their own God.

Daniel 3

Now, there came a time when King
Nebuchadnezzar built a gold statue 90 feet tall
and 9 feet wide,
Requiring his kingdom's subjects and peoples in
his statue and his gods abide.

For at the sound of every horn, zither, lyre, pipe,
and flute,
All peoples, regardless of race, language or
nation, were to bow and salute.

The statue, which Nebuchadnezzar set up,
Was not to persuade or disrupt

Belief Shadrach, Meshach and Abednego of their
God
With each required nod.

Brought before the king,
They acknowledged their refusal to do the
required royal thing.

And after defying once again in earnest,
They were bound and thrown into the fiery
furnace.

Shadrach, Meshach, and Abednego stated their
God would save them from the fire.
And if not, they'd never bow to another god, even
in times so dire.

Fuming with rage, the king ordered the furnace hotter seven times,
Only to kill the escorting soldiers attempting to execute these for their admitted crimes.

But King Nebuchadnezzar called others out to see:
Four men in the furnace he saw, not three!

He then ordered the three to come on out.
Not a singed hair or thread was burned or scorched throughout.

So he issued a new command
Throughout all the land:

"If any people defy
The God of these three and question why,

"They'd be torn limb to limb, and their houses would be emphatically gone."
These three were then promoted to even higher positions within Babylon.

It finally came to Nebuchadnezzar,
That the God of Israel, of these from afar,
Is greater than any other god by far.

(We are not so high as to wonder why,
That whenever God has a plan, He will use every
flawed kind of man,
And change their life around, making it
righteously sound.
Such may be the case with Nebuchadnezzar,
here in Daniel, Chapter 4.
Unlike the statue of Daniel 2 and 3, this is
Nebuchadnezzar's dream about a tree.)

Unknown: Illustrator of 'L 'Histoire du Vieux et
du Nouveau Testament; Nicolas Fontaine
(author), 1670

Daniel 4

His praises run high
Of the God Most High

With comfort and prosperity,
One night a dream frightened him terribly.

After consulting all his wise and noble men,
Daniel finally arrived for him to confide in.

King Nebuchadnezzar tells of the dream of his
sleep.
Again, a forward-looking peep.

A great and mighty tree was in the middle of the ground,
Reaching to heaven and seen by the earth all around.

The tree with fresh green leaves, loaded with fruit for all to eat, had shade for wild animals and branches for birds' nests,
When a messenger came down from heaven where God rests.

"Cut down the tree, chop off the branches," the messenger shouted.
"Shake off the leaves, scatter the fruits so the animals and birds will be routed."

"Leave the stump and roots in the ground,
Iron and bronze will be tied, with green grass all around."

"Let the dew of heaven drench
Live like an animal wench
So life won't be a cinch."

"This has been declared: We all are in need,
And from God's purposes can't be freed."

"Tell me, Belteshazzar," said Nebuchadnezzar,
"let God tell you now,
The who, where, when and how."

Daniel injected: "That tree you see is you, a greatness that reaches the heavens above,
To the ends of the earth, God's showing His love."

"A suffering end to your earthly prosperity
Will come with you driven from human society.

"You will live and eat with the animals all
around
And crawl among the fields with them on the
ground.

"And the morning dew will drench you,
Until realization as to what is true.

"The God Most high rules over kings and
kingdoms,
And He chooses who will lead them.

"The stump and the roots means you'll receive
your kingdom again
When it is learned that such power is not self-
attained."

Daniel ended with a plea:
"Please, listen to me.

"Stop sinning and do what is right, break from
your wicked past and help the poor.
Otherwise, this dream becomes reality for sure."

And it came to pass,
The dream's fulfillment at last.

A year later, during self-glorification of a city so
great,
Nebuchadnezzar attained the guarantee of the
predicted demise of late.

After his seven periods time had passed,
He praised and worshipped the Most High God
at last.

"I will honor, praise, and glorify the king of
heaven, for His acts are just and true, and the
proud will be humbled," Nebuchadnezzar said,
as a greater honor returned to him
When God eventually restored his kingdom.

"Daniel Interpreting the Writing on the Wall" by Gustave Doré

Dan 5:5-6 ...and the king saw the part of the hand that wrote. Then the king's countenance was changed, and his thoughts troubled him, ... and his knees smote one against another.

Daniel 5

It came to pass, a number of years later, after
King Nebuchadnezzar,
That a great feast was given to thousands of
nobles by King Belshazzar.

While drinking merrily various and numerous
bottles of wines
With his noblemen, wives, and concubines,

The king ordered the use of the gold and silver
cups from Jerusalem's Temple of God,
Brought by way when upon Babylon land King
Nebuchadnezzar trod.

During their worshipping of idols of silver, gold,
bronze, iron, wood, and stone,
They saw a sight which scared them to the bone.

The king was knee-knocking pale with fright,
A terrifying hand on the wall as it did write.

So he called all the wise men on Babylon
To help read this writing upon the wall apron.

But no one was able to translate the sight,
For even they were frightened an ashen white.

But the Queen mother hurried to the banquet
hall
To inform the king of a man filled with great
knowledge, the spirit and all.

He is one who could possibly interpret this sight,
Because the spirit of the holy gods had given
him wisdom, understanding, and insight.

Not interested in the robes of purple and the
gifts of highest beings,
Daniel answered, "Keep the gifts or give them to
others, but I'll tell you the meanings."

"The Most High God," stated Daniel, "allowed
your predecessor
Sovereignty, majesty, glory, and honor. His
name was Nebuchadnezzar."

"He had been a ruthless, fearful man,
But God had a plan."

"His heart was hardened with pride
Upon which all his earthly royal throne and
riches did ride."

Daniel continued, "He was driven from society
To become a human among animal notoriety,

"To eat grass as a cow; live among the donkeys;
drenched with dew from the sky
Until he learned the God Most High

"Rules the world's kingdoms,
And appoints anyone he desires to rule over
them.

"You, O Belshazzar, have not yet humbled
yourself,
Drinking and worshipping idols with gold and
silver cups from the Temple of God's shelf

"Honoring not the God of your breath
Will surely lead to your ultimate and timely
death.

"The writing on thee wall
Precedes your fall:

"*Mene* – your days of reign are numbered; *Tekel*
– you have been weighed and have failed," the
message written,
"*Parsin* – your kingdom will be divided between
the Medes and Persians."

Daniel was promoted to the third highest in all
the land,
And dying that night, King Belshazzar, his fate
left to understand.

"Daniel in the Den of Lions" *by Gustave Doré*

Dan 6:20-21 ...*and* the king spake and said to Daniel, O Daniel, servant of the living God, is thy God, whom thou servest continually, able to deliver thee from the lions? Then said Daniel unto the king, O king, live for ever.

Daniel 6

In the years to follow, King Darius
Divided the kingdom into 120 provinces.

Daniel, along with two others, were each made
an administrator,
The king wanting to later appoint him a top
coordinator.

Always faithful, honest, and responsible to the
end,
Daniel had adversaries to find fault only with his
religion.

So they set out to have the king sign a new law:
Praying to anyone, human or divine, except to
the king, would be a deadly flaw.

Thrown into the lion's den
Will be for anyone guilty of this sin.

About this, Daniel went to pray,
Just as he did three times a day.

Only this time, the accusers wanting his
downfall reported this,
As his demise was their deepest wish.

Because he praised his God and the new law he
failed to obey,
His enemies found reason to have him taken
away.

But Darius, upset with the law he'd sent,
Wished he could find a way to get Daniel out of
this predicament.

However, no law signed by the king back then
Could be withdrawn or rewritten
King Darius fasted all night and wished of
Daniel's God
To save him from where the hungry lions trod.

But early one morning came
With things not quite the same.

King Darius called out,
"Daniel, are you about?"

And then to the king's ears ring,
Daniel exclaimed, "Long live the king!"

"God has shut the mouth of every beast,
So upon me they couldn't feast."

King Darius then ordered thrown into the den
Daniel's accusers, their wives and children.

Those who accused so maliciously
Were then devoured and consumed ferociously.

Darius sent a message to his kingdom's people:
"Before the God of Daniel, everyone should
tremble."

"He is the Living God, and He will endure
forever.
His kingdom and rule will be ever and ever."

"He rescues and saves people, performing
miraculous signs of wonder
In the heavens and the earth, under."

Rescued and saved from the lions' power,
And under this king, God allowed Daniel to
prosper.

"The Vision of the Four Beasts" by Gustave Doré

Dan 7:2-3 Daniel spake and said, I saw in my vision by night, and, behold, the four winds of the heaven strove upon the great sea. And four great beasts came up from the sea, diverse one from another...

Daniel 7

Way back when King Belshazzar reigned
Even Daniel had dreams and visions and not
understanding
A great storm in the sea churned,
Strong winds blowing in every direction.

Upon my eyes did feast,
Out of the water came four huge ugly beasts.

And I must say,
They differed in each and every way.

Like a lion with eagle's wings,
Which were torn away, and it stood on two feet
and had a mind like a human being.

The second looked like a bear,
Rearing up on one side, three ribs in its mouth
ready to tear.

And a voice said to it, "Get up, with all your
power
Many people may you devour."

The beast from the sea
Was given this great authority.

With four wings upon its back,
It looked like a leopard ready to attack.

Then in my vision that night,
The fourth beast gave a horrifying fright.

Terrifying, dreadful and very strong,
Victims didn't last very long.

This beast had 10 horns in all,
But three were wrenched out, making room for a
new horn, small.

The little horn, with eyes and a mouth looking
very humanly,
Started boasting very arrogantly.

Whitest of white, did I see, with clothes like
snow shown,
And hair the whitest wool was upon the Ancient
One, as He sat upon the throne.

He sat among a throne of fire,
With hundreds of millions of angels ready to
administer and admire.

The court began its session.
Listen now to hear the lesson:

The one with the littlest horns, the fourth beast,
Boasting loudly caused it to be the first of the
fire's feast.

Destroyed right before them all,
A mighty Judge will also author the last three
authorities to fall.

Continuing with my vision as it did happen,
A man came from the clouds of Heaven,

Approaching the Ancient One.
(Was this God's Son?)

He was given all authority, honor, and royal
power over all,
His rule eternal to never fall.

Troubled by this vision,
I asked for interpretation.

"The four beasts," I was told,
"Are the four kingdoms of the world to take hold.

"These four would lead the earth
But in the end, the Most High will come and give
his people their worth.

"The fourth beast, the most terrifying,
Started crushing its victims and devouring.

"The little horn that replaced the now rooted and
out
Represents now a greatness trying its hold
throughout.

"Waging war against the people of the Most High
Until the Ancient One was to arrive.

"The fourth beast, 10 horns in all, looking to
rule the world's empire,
Will finally not acquire.

"The court will take away the beast's authority
And give the holy people sovereignty.

To rule forever
And ever."

The vision came to a close.

Unknown: Master Connected to the Protestant
Reformation Era Writings

Daniel 8

Unlike the previous vision I had during
Belshazzar's year one
The vision I had during the third was not fun.

While standing beside
The Ulai River wide,

A ram with two horns appeared,
One horn longer than the other as it neared.

West, north, and south, all things were butted
out of the way.
No victims could guard against it; it was having
a great day!

Then swiftly from the west came a between-the-
eyes one-horned goat charging the ram,
Causing the two horns to be knocked off with
the slam.

The goat eventually became full of power
Until the very hour

When the horn fell off and was replaced with
four new horns, prominent.
But from one horn came one, small, yet very
dominant.

It went south and east to Israel,
Its power reaching all places between heaven's
stars and hell.

Attacking and destroying the Temple of God,
This mighty army was permitted to pillage and
trod.

Sacrilege, destruction, again and again,
But God allowed no other to attack and destroy
for this sin.

I then heard a holy one say,
"How long will it be this way?

 "How long until the restoration of the Temple of
God,
And this army upon the beaten earth be allowed
to trod?"

The other holy one answered, "In twenty three
hundred days and nights,
Only then will the Temple of God be made right."

As I tried to understand the dream,
A voice called a name,

"Gabriel, tell this man
His dream to understand."

Terrified as Gabriel approached me,
I fainted and fell upon my belly and knees.

He referred to me as Son of Man,
And related that I must understand

Visions relating to the end of time,
Given me with meanings sublime.

Gabriel touched me and helped me to my feet, still in shock,
Stating what has been revealed is the end of this planet rock.

"The kings of Media and Persia, represented by the two-horned ram
Was charged by the King of Greece, the goat which slammed.

"Four horns replacing the one large is the Greek Empire with four equal sections,
When a fierce king lets loose with a shuttering hail of destruction.

"This king will be successful in all that he does,
Deception, destruction, and attacking are the buzz.

"The Prince of princes is to take him on,
But that's when he, too, will be broken.

"Twenty three hundred days is true."
I became sick, sleepless, with lack of understanding greatly troubling me, this vision to get through.

" The man Gabriel . . . touched me about the time of the evening oblation." – *Dan.* ix. 21.

Daniel 9

During the first year of King Darius' reign,
From writings of the prophets, great insights I
gained.

The Word of the Lord, through Jeremiah, from
which I learned,
Jerusalem lying desolate for 70 years is my
concern.

So I pleaded with my Lord God, in prayer and
while fasting,
Wearing sackcloth and sprinkled ashen.

I will lift you up, Lord God, always fulfilling
promises and things you commanded.
But having rebelled, not followed your rules,
fallen to the ground we have landed.

Lord, you are just and right, our faces hide in
shame.
True, wherever you have driven us, our
disloyalty is to blame.

We have not followed your laws, though all-
forgiving and merciful you are to Israel.
But we have sinned, and many times, sin
prevailed.

The judgment of the law of Moses comes
because we don't obey,
For all you want is for us from sin to turn away.

We have not seen the truth in order to be free,
And every curse written has come to be.

We have not shown righteousness,
And have sinned, full of wickedness.

I know, our situation is sad.
We have sinned, our ancestors bad.

Neighbors mock us as we plead.
God, help us be freed!

Open your eyes.
Observe our wretchedness.

Your city in ruins lies,
But your mercy is what our request tries.

Hear, forgive, listen, and act.
We are desperate, and that's a fact!

I prayed, pleading and confessin'
With God for Jerusalem, His Holy mountain.

Again, like in a previous vision, a command
Brought Gabriel to help me understand.

Gabriel said, "God loves you so much,
And He wants you to understand the vision as
such."

A time period of 70 sets of seven
Decreed to put down rebellion

To atone for guilt, to bring an end to sin;
To bring righteousness, confirming the prophet's
vision.

Seven plus 62 sets of seven will pass in stride
From the command to rebuild Jerusalem until
the Anointed One arrives.

Even with all the perilous tenseness,
Jerusalem will rebuild with streets and strong
defenses.

And after the 62 sets of seven, the Anointed One
will be killed,
Leaving some people thrilled.

A ruler will rise to destroy the city and the
Temple of God will descend.
War and its miseries will be until the very end.

He'll rule for a time, setting up an object of
sacrilegion
And one that causes desecration.

Until, with all his terrible deeds
On this defiler, the end will be decreed.

Unknown: Illustrator of Henry Davenport
Northrup's "Treasures of the Bible." (1894)

Unknown: Master Connected to the Protestant
Reformation Era Writings

Daniel 10

In the third year of King Cyrus' reign,
Another vision came.

Times of war and great hardship, along with
other future events,
But this time, Daniel understood what was
meant.

The vision came to me,
While standing beside the Tigris River,
mourning, sober, and meat-free.

On April 23, 536 B.C.,
I saw a man standing next to me.

Those along with me ran and left me alone.
My body became weak, my face pale as a stone.

I then heard him speak.
I fainted, face to the ground, from my feet.

A hand touched me,
Lifting me to my hands and knees.

"Greatly loved by God, listen to what I have to
say.
I've been sent to answer the request you pray.

"For 21 days, on my way here, I was hampered
by the spirit of Kingdom Persia, when
Michael arrived to help me then.

"Having left Michael with the spirit of the Persian Kingdom,
I came here to tell future things for your people are to come."

I couldn't say a word,
Looking at the ground, face-to-face with my Lord.

I'm frightened by the vision,
How can someone like me receive such attention?

He again touched and comforted me, giving strength anew.
I felt strong again, speaking the truth now, "Be through!"

"Do you know why I came to see you?
To tell what is true.

"I must soon depart, to fight the spirit of the Persian Kingdom
And then the one from the Greek Kingdom.

"Michael helps me, your spirit prince.
I have helped him since the first year of Darius, as support and defense."

Daniel 11

Then, three more Persian kings will reign,
But the fourth may have seemed insane.

Because of riches and political advantages he
bore,
He'll stir conflict with the kingdom of Greece to
war.

A mighty king then will come to reign,
Succeeding at all he will try to attain.

But at the pinnacle of his power,
His kingdom into four parts will shower.

Ruled not by any royal descendents,
Nor have any authority since.

The king of the south will have an official
beneath
Who becomes more powerful to rule with great
strength.

The daughter of the south's king
Will be given to the north's, wedding bells ring.

Given to effect alliance,
Over him, though, she will lose influence.

But a relative of hers will lead the south,
Only to raise an army, attack and beat the north
about.

He'll carry back with him to Egypt idols and
priceless things,
Leaving alone for some years the north king.

Back and forth great trials the kingdoms fought
Assembling mighty armies, attacking, some left
not able to endure the on-slaught.

The lawless ones among your own
Will join to fulfill the vision song.

North will march south and pause in Israel
And after an alliance, a daughter to infiltrate;
this plan will also fail.

Coastal cities will come under attack
But a foreign commander will repel them back.

A power will come, but not in royal succession,
Slipping in when least expected.

A deceitful man will he be,
Allying with the many others, mainly the greedy.

He'll enter the land of the riches to plunder,
Handing over the wealth to his followers and
friends, and those under.

He'll raise an army to go against the south,
A mighty army, too, no doubt.

Plotted within for the other's downfall,
Each king at the conference table's call.

Lie, deceive, in each and every way.
Makes no difference, though, the end will still
come on time and in the appointed way.

The north king going home with the spoils of
war,
Alienating himself against those of the covenant
adore.

At the invasion of the north again,
Western warships will run off, these of the
northern land.

But he will vent anger against the people of the
holy covenant,
By taking up four events:

Taking over the Temple fortress: polluting the
sanctuary; stopping the daily sacrifice; and
setting up the sacrilegious object.
He plans to flatter and win over many a-subject.

Those who violate the covenant will go to his
side,
But the strong knowing God, with Him will resist
and abide.

The wise, the teachers and such, giving others
daily instruction
Will die as a result of persecution.

They'll be refined, cleansed and made pure,
For the end will come for sure.

The king, a blasphemer before God,
Will over all succeed, with no regard upon whom
he will trod.

And then at the end, the king of the south will
attack,
But the north will violently fight back.

Many countries will he capture,
And gold, silver, and other treasures of Egypt
conquer.

Libyans and Ethiopians, alike, will be servants
To those of the covenant.

The news from the east and north flow,
But great anger of the north grows.

Stopping between the sea and the glorious holy
mountain, a tent will be pitched.
But while there, time runs out, and none to help
be unhitched.

Daniel 12

Archangel Michael, who guards your nation
Will arrive, and great anguish will be since any
city's creation.

And those written in the book will have
everlasting life,
While eternal contempt will be for those filled
with strife.

Those who are wise will shine like the sky,
And those who helped turn away from wicked
ways will, like stars, shine.

But Daniel, this prophesy a secret keep,
As many go and come, with knowledge increase.

And I saw two others across the river, on the
opposite bank sides.
One asked, "How long with these crushing
events must we abide?"

The other, dressed in linen, raised his hands to
heaven and answered, "It will go on for awhile,
and when

the shattering of the holy people will end,
All these things will have happened."

I heard, but understood not, so I asked what it
meant,
"Lord, how will the end be sent?"

But He said, "Go, for this is for the end.
Many will be cleansed, purified and refined, but
the wicked still won't understand."

From the set up of the sacrilegious object and
daily sacrifice is taken away
There will be 1290 days, but bless those
remaining to the end of the 1335th day.

For you, Daniel, go your own way until the end,
To receive your inheritance when you rise again.

"All these things shall be finished."—*Dan.* xii. 7.

www.ingramcontent.com/pod-product-compliance
Lightning Source LLC
Chambersburg PA
CBHW031335040426
42443CB00005B/351